Helping Young Children Develop Through Play

A Practical Guide for Parents, Caregivers, and Teachers

Janet K. Sawyers and Cosby S. Rogers

National Association for the
Education of Young Children
Washington, D.C.

Photo credits: Ann-Marie Mott iv; Marietta Lynch 2, 32, 51; Marianne Montero 6, 41; Cheryl Namkung 9; Robert Godwin 11; Michael Siluk 13; Marilyn Nolt 15; Janice Mason 17; Nancy Alexander 19, 28, 53, 54; Faith Bowlus 21; Michael Ungerleider 22; Francis Wardle 26; Robert Koenig 34; Barbara Brockman 38; Subjects & Predicates 42; Mary Ellen Powers 46; Cleo Freelance Photo 48; Rick Reinhard 56.

National Association for the Education of Young Children
1509 16th Street, NW
Washington, DC 20036-1426
800-424-2460 or 202-232-8777
www.naeyc.org

Second printing, 1990. Third printing, 1992. Fourth printing, 1994. Fifth printing, 1998. Sixth printing, 2001.

Through its publications program the National Association for the Education of Young Children (NAEYC) provides a forum for discussion of major issues and ideas in the early childhood field, with the hope of provoking thought and promoting professional growth. The views expressed or implied are not necessarily those of the Association. NAEYC thanks the authors, who donated much time and effort to develop this book as a contribution to the profession.

Library of Congress Control Number: 88-06213

ISBN 0-935989-24-2

NAEYC #345

Design and production: Jack Zibulsky

Printed in the United States of America.

Contents

The Importance of Play

Kelly's mother beamed when her 3-year-old showed her a
large scribble and announced, "That says Kelly." "I'm so glad
you're starting to teach handwriting," the mother said to Kelly's
teacher. "I worry about her just playing all day."

" Just playing." When we hear those words applied
to a young child, we know that once again someone
has misunderstood the nature of a child's life and learning.
How has this misunderstanding occurred?

Our society has become very complicated, competitive,
and hurried. As a result, children's free play is being replaced
with structured activities at home, in child care settings, and
in the schools. This practice reflects an earnest desire by
parents and teachers to provide what is best for the child.
We all want children to compete successfully in our
complex, hurry-up world. However, the hurried, structured,
work-oriented approach is based on several faulty and
unwarranted beliefs, namely that:

- earlier is better,
- adult-directed work is the best way for children to learn,
  and
- play has little value.

A cycle of frustration, failure, and lack of interest in
learning can result when children's early experiences are
not developmentally appropriate or when they have little
or no relation to the children's interests, needs, and goals.

When children learn through play, they learn to enjoy learning.

As adults, we are often reluctant to give children control over the learning situation. Many of us are more comfortable when we are directly teaching than when we act as facilitators for children's play. But we must allow children to play if they are to enjoy learning.

In play, children are much freer to master new knowledge at their own rate and in their own way. This reduces the tension and anxiety that can inhibit learning. Thus, in play learning is fun and worry free. When children are engaged in play, they are learning and enjoying every minute of it.

On the surface, children's play looks simple. In fact, play touches on every aspect of development and learning. Therefore, any program that claims to offer more than "just play" is ignoring what many researchers have found out about how young children learn and develop.

How does play relate to other behavior?

One indication of the value of play is that the failure of a child to engage in progressively more complex and elaborate play behaviors may be an indication of problems in cognitive, social, physical, or emotional development (Tizard, 1977).

Research and theory about how young children learn show us that play contributes to children's development in a number of ways:

1. Play provides the opportunity for children to practice new cognitive, social-emotional, and physical skills. As they master these skills, they can use them in other situations. Babies learn to turn the pages of a book and begin to sense a sequence to the story. Books become a lifelong source of enjoyment when children begin to learn about them in a playful manner.

2. Play offers numerous opportunities for children to act on objects and experience events. Each field trip, each friendship built with children and adults (including some from different cultures), and each experience in building with blocks builds understanding about the world.

3. Play is an active form of learning that unites the mind, body, and spirit (Levy, 1978). Until at least the age of 9, children's learning occurs best when the whole self is involved. Watch how absorbed children are when they paint at an easel, work on a puzzle, or gaze into another's eyes.

4. Play enables children to use their real experiences to organize concepts of how the world operates. For example, during a bowling game children may decide to keep count of how many pins each knocks down by keeping tokens or paper clips in a pile; older children may want to write the numbers on paper. Children's first attempts to read and write frequently occur during play.

5. Through play, children can see how new experiences are related to previous learning. Much of what we learn cannot be taught directly but must be put together in our own way through our experiences. We all know the feeling of "Ah-ha!" when something finally clicks.

6. As they play, children can develop a playful attitude— an attitude toward inventiveness that contributes to being able to think up many ideas, new ways to do things, and ways to solve problems. Children are open to a variety of solutions. They are quite inventive in solving problems such as how to delay taking a nap.

7. Art appreciation develops through play. When children make clay pots, they become potters. As they play with words, they develop a sense for the rhythm and sound of poetry and prose.

8. Play enables children to learn about learning—through curiosity, invention, staying with the task, and in a host of other ways. Children's attention spans are amazingly long when they are interested. They are spellbound as they watch ants in an anthill; they keep trying until the puzzle is solved; they delight in recognizing their own names for the first time. Children become interested in learning when they learn through play. What's more, they learn to like learning when they learn through play because it feels so satisfying.

9. Play reduces the tension that often comes with having to achieve or needing to learn. In play, adults do not interfere. Children relax. Play challenges yet does not punish for mistakes.

10. Through playing with peers, children develop skills for seeing something from another person's point of view, cooperating, helping, and sharing, as well as for solving problems. They develop both leading and following behaviors, both of which we need to get along well as adults. Such experiences help children think about their social world and gain an understanding of themselves.

11. Children express and work out emotional aspects of everyday experiences as well as frightening events, especially through dramatic play. They delight in taking the powerful role of the doctor as they give the teacher a shot.

Every aspect of a child's life is interwoven with play. This is the nature of a child. As adults, how do we preserve and encourage the natural activity of play?

Every aspect of a child's life is interwoven with play.

THE IMPORTANCE OF PLAY

What Can Adults Do To Support Play?

To play, children and adults alike need a certain attitude or feeling and they need an environment that supports and encourages play. Adults who have a playful attitude and who appreciate playful children are able to encourage them to develop fully through play. Adults who work with children need to be aware of what they can do to provide the proper environment for play. We will describe the general principles that adults should follow to support play. We will also list specific suggestions for supporting play at various developmental levels.

General principles for supporting play

• Let children choose their activity. Provide a variety of toys, activities, and materials, but let children decide which ones to explore and use in play.

• Let children determine how long they will play. Pushing children to continue with an activity that no longer holds their interest is likely to lead them to avoid that activity next time. Also, interrupting them before they've finished interferes with the development of attention span. Pre-schoolers need notification that play time will end in 2 minutes or 5 minutes so they can finish up.

- Provide activities and materials that challenge various levels of skills. Challenges make play more interesting. When we let children choose their activities, they usually choose ones that hold a challenge for them. If there is a variety from which to choose, they can choose the one that is just right—not too easy and not too difficult. If a child chooses an activity that adults think is "too easy," it means that the child knows something we don't: Either the child needs more practice with the skills involved, or the child needs to repeat the familiar to develop confidence before feeling up to the next challenge.

- Make sure the physical environment is safe. This means that toys and materials must be safe and appropriate for each age. Outdoor playgrounds must be safe in order for children to feel free to practice new large motor skills.

- Arrange space so as to minimize interruptions. Use low shelves or enclosed spaces to divide areas so that children from one area are not as likely to interrupt others.

- Allow children to use objects and try out new skills in unusual ways. As long as the variation is safe and affordable and does not damage property or hurt someone, the value of learning through play outweighs the merits of doing things the usual way just for the sake of tradition. Experimenting with new ways to do things is a source of invention.

- Plan the schedule so that children get the most from their play. Children who are tired, hungry, or hurried can't play. Plan for long and unhurried play times, rest, and nourishment; alternate periods of active and quiet play.

Let children choose which materials to use and, as long as their choices are safe and considerate, how to use them.

When children are pretending

• Always allow choice—never require pretend play.

• Unless children are playing dangerously, it is usually best to allow them to act out even negative scenes. Children often use pretense as an opportunity to do what they are not allowed to do in reality. For example, Lisa's teacher observed her as she pretended to put the baby (doll) in the oven. Four-year-olds often blow up ships and forts. Observe these acts and try to determine what meaning they have for the child.

• Allow children to enact roles and events differently than they are done in real life. Young preschoolers act out roles they observe in their daily lives as they participate in sociodramatic play. Older preschoolers may invent unusual characters—such as monsters and flying robots—that are fantastic works of the imagination. Why not have a birthday cake with presents baked in the middle? Why not invent buses that fly, boats that can sprout wings, or good monsters that cure chicken pox with ice cream? Why not rearrange traditional stories? Three kindergartners put on a revised version of *The Three Bears* called *The Three Humans*. There were three humans and one dog with black hair, named Blackilocks.

• Supply props for themes of interest to each developmental level.

• Provide the stimulus for pretense by arranging experiences the children share—going on field trips, having visitors to the school, reading books, and occasionally seeing a movie or stage play.

• Participate when needed, observe when not. Sometimes children need adults to help them find a new theme or think of a new event for a drama or artistic work they are producing repeatedly without novel innovations. The adult may be needed as an actor to help fill in. Or the adult can help isolated, shy, or rejected children enter the play by suggesting a role for them or offering them a prized prop to bring to the group. At other times, adults contribute best by allowing child-directed expressions to continue without adult dominance. Use those times for observing.

Challenge the level of play by suggesting more abstract props as substitutions. Sometimes this means putting away more realistic props or suggesting themes that will require the construction of props from art materials.

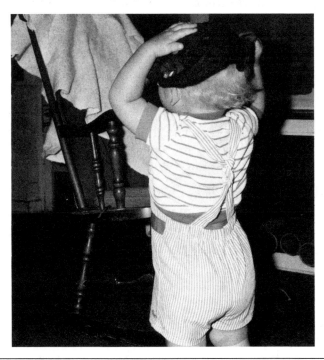

When children are making or building

• Focus on the process, not the product. Comment on how children have combined pieces or mixed colors, how the materials feel in the hands, or how much fun it was to make up the song. Do not use models for children to copy—no patterns to cut out, no dittos, and no coloring books. Do not make a play dough model or draw a picture and expect children to make one like it.

• Do not use competitions to compare products. This takes the focus off the process and inhibits children from attempting to risk new ways of doing things.

• Give children the freedom to be messy. Show them it is OK by allowing yourself to get messy. Enjoy the smoothness of fingerpaint, the squishiness of pudding, the feel of mud. Provide clean-up supplies—sponges, soap, water, brooms—and comment during cleanup that the fun was worth it. (Children usually find this kind of cleaning up fun too, as opposed to picking up a hundred blocks or puzzle pieces.) Encourage parents to dress children in clothing that is easily cleaned so they don't have to be concerned about getting messy. Dress yourself so that it's OK for you to be messy too. Provide smocks for activities that might permanently damage clothing.

• Provide more materials as children grow older. Three or four selections for a collage may be ample for 3-year-olds, but older children need a larger variety; toddlers enjoy one or two colors of paint, but older children need more.

Helping Babies Play

Birth to 4 months

In these early months, babies explore their new world with their eyes. Things you can do to help this exploration are:

• Provide bright, moving objects for babies to practice looking at. Mobiles should be interesting from the baby's view. Provide consistency by leaving the objects in their place so the baby begins to recognize familiar objects in the crib at home as well as in out-of-home care settings.

• Move objects close to and away from babies. Also, move your face close to and away from them. This will make a different visual impact than things that stay still. It helps babies judge the relationship between objects and between themselves and objects.

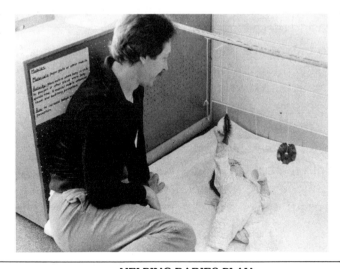

Young infants need plenty of interesting things to look at—especially their caregiver's expressive face.

- Hold babies up to your shoulder and move them around to provide a better view.
- Show the baby in a mirror how beautiful and wonderful he is.
- Playfully engage the baby in repetitions of looking, smiling, talking, and laughing. The adult usually starts the game by smiling and talking to gain baby's attention. Experienced caregivers and mothers find that tongue clicking, head shaking, moving quickly toward baby and then stopping, and repeating certain sounds are entertaining to babies. Perform in a clown-like fashion and stop to wait for baby to do her part—laughing, smiling, or moving her arms and legs in excitement. Repeat the clown show several times, each time stopping for baby to have a turn. The show stops when baby starts to look away, or shows other signs of fatigue, overstimulation, or lack of interest.

Babies explore sound and motion too. Some suggestions for increasing these explorations are:

- Talk to babies in a playful way. Smile and repeat soft sounds—again, again. Stop between sounds and watch for them to smile or move in response to your voice. If you get a playful response, repeat the show.
- Sing to the baby. Make up songs just for this baby.
- Dance with the baby nestled on your shoulder.
- Play with the baby's hands and feet, gently patting and rubbing, saying silly, soft sounds to match. "Pedal" the baby's legs for a bike ride, describing where you're going.

Four to 8 months

In this stage, infants can use not only eyes and ears but hands and mouth to explore objects. Some ideas for this age group's play are:

• Keep toy safety a primary concern. Provide objects that can be held by small hands but that are not small enough to fit entirely in the mouth. Toys must be washable and made of tough, durable materials. There must be no sharp edges or points that can injure and no small parts that can come off—small wheels or buttons, for example.

• Toys that move or make a sound in response to the baby's actions are best. Look for toys that pop up, turn, honk, rattle, or play music when the baby pushes, punches, hits, or pokes at them.

• Minimize interruptions to protect babies' exploration of new objects. Watch but don't interrupt when babies are busy exploring. Also prevent other children (especially older ones) from interrupting play. Having duplicates of several toys will help prevent would-be "snatchers" from robbing the explorer.

Babies are also becoming more social and enjoy your efforts to entertain them by:

• playing "This Little Piggy Went to Market" with their toes and

• singing special songs while changing diapers and clothes, or cutting nails.

Let babies explore with all their senses. Provide toys that are safe to mouth and that respond to the child's manipulations.

Eight to 12 months

Babies now are fully active in exploring their world. Almost all babies crawl or creep; many walk around the room holding on, some are independently walking. Babies now combine objects, and practice dropping, throwing, and squeezing. Some suggestions for fostering their play are:

• Provide objects to put in containers and dump out. Some good containers are plastic bowls, plastic storage boxes, baskets, and shoe boxes. Make sure that items to put in the containers are small enough for small hands but not small enough to fit entirely in the mouth. Good things to put in are small blocks, yarn balls, plastic lids, and rings from stack-a-ring toys.

• Hide objects for baby to find. Hide objects under covers. At first, leave part of the toy visible or cover with a see-through material (thin scarf, plastic lid, cheese cloth). Hide the baby under a cover—look and look until baby pops out, while asking, "Where's the baby? Where's Lucy?"

• Help babies practice sounds by repeating their sounds back—for example, *dada, oh oh,* and by the end of the first year, words like *kitty, baby,* and *doll.* Don't limit speech to imitating babies but extend and expand their words into sentences.

• Read to the baby.

• Provide toys that challenge the infant's skills. Children this age practice pulling, pushing, poking, punching.

• Be sure toys are in working order. Toys that don't work are just no fun. They can be very frustrating.

• Introduce toys with more than one part. Infants this age especially like things that fit inside something else.

18   **HELPING BABIES PLAY**

As they approach their first birthdays, children appreciate toys with more than one part.

- Stretch baby's arms above her head, asking, "How big is baby? Soooo big!" After a while, baby will hold her arms up alone to respond to your question.
- Play Pat-a-Cake, Peek-a-Boo, and Copycat with the baby.
- Children in this age group enjoy the sensory feeling of moving through space—riding piggyback, swinging in child-seat swings, riding in wagons, and dancing in an adult's arms. They and older babies also enjoy bouncing on an adult's knee to the accompaniment of a song or verse such as "This Is the Way the Lady Rides."

Twelve to 18 months

Infants in this age group are great experimenters, trying out all their skills this way and that just to see what will happen. The first pretend play occurs in this group when infants begin to act "as if" doing daily activities. They pretend to sleep, eat, or bathe. They then apply these acts to others and later copy others' behaviors as their own. Some suggestions for supporting play for these babies are:

• Provide simple pictures of familiar items (laminated, covered with clear plastic, or put into zip-type plastic bags) for baby to practice naming.

• Read to the baby, talking about the book as you go.

• Provide safe places (indoors and outdoors) for moving— walking and climbing. Due to the likelihood of many falls, climbing steps should be plastic or covered with carpet. Tunnels and cabinets provide opportunities for going in, out, through, and under.

• Be the receiver of the child's pretend actions. Take a drink from the empty cup, smack your lips, and say, "Ummmm, good." Let the child comb your hair or pretend to wash your face. Then extend the pretense to another recipient such as a doll. Support the child's language development by narrating the drama as it progresses: "Jimmy is asleep," or "Oh, I'm going to be clean. I'm getting a bath."

• Provide real-looking toys for daily activities such as eating, bathing, riding, and cleaning. Important toys for pretense at this age are:

Toddlers begin to appreciate pictures and to pretend with realistic props.

Dolls (realistic, representative of a variety of racial/ethnic groups)

Daddy	Brother/Sister
Mommy	Baby

Transportation vehicles

boats	planes
cars	trains

Toddlers enjoy practicing large- and small-muscle skills.

HELPING TODDLERS PLAY

Helping Toddlers Play: Eighteen Months to 3 Years

Toddlers strive for independence as they practice skills they can carry out themselves. Their newfound independence is expressed in a need for choice within limits. Ideas for fostering their play are:

• Provide equipment to challenge gross motor skills. Toddlers enjoy pushing toy lawn mowers, riding large toy trucks and cars, rocking the rocking boat, climbing stairs, sliding down a short slide, and crawling through tunnels. Large and small balls to throw and catch are a must.

• Provide objects/materials to challenge fine motor skills. Toddlers enjoy stacking and nesting materials, lids to put on and take off, simple wooden puzzles with knobs, and pounding benches. They enjoy practicing dressing skills on dolls or dressing frames (large snaps, zippers, large buttons). Boxes that can be opened by turning a knob, moving a slide, or lifting a hook are also challenging.

• Provide objects that relate in some way—blocks to stack, lids to put on containers, simple whole-piece puzzles.

• Make sure all toy materials are in working order. Do the snaps snap? Are all puzzle pieces there? Is there a nesting cup missing?

• Provide duplicates of play materials. Toddlers enjoy playing near familiar playmates, but they are not likely to share materials. They need to possess what is "mine"; this is not "selfishness," but rather an important step in the development of a sense of self.

• Keep group size small in order to minimize interruptions and to provide the security that comes from having familiar, trusted people in the environment. Toddlers who seem independent one minute may need a warm lap to sit in the next minute.

• Let children choose from the variety of toys and material provided. Do not rotate toddlers from one activity to another on a set schedule or insist that they try something that does not interest them.

• Allow children to try new skills in their own way. Joy tried riding the Big Wheel by getting on backwards. She soon discovered that it didn't work very well. Her teacher did not direct the play by insisting that Joy try to do it "right." The teacher allowed her to discover on her own what worked best.

• Provide large soft blocks for stacking and knocking down. Supply nesting materials and other stacking materials.

• Allow opportunities for water play and manipulating soft play dough. Because sand is likely to get into the eyes at this age, try other materials such as grits or rice. Color the rice for a little variety. Use pudding for finger paint and soft, squishy dough instead of mud. Be open to the variety of materials that toddlers can safely manipulate (remember they are still likely to taste their creations).

• Be sure that any building materials, puzzle pieces, or manipulatives are large enough that they will not fit entirely into the mouth; toddlers can choke.

When toddlers are pretending, they need realistic objects to play with. In addition to dolls and transportation objects, listed in the 12 to 18 months section, toddlers enjoy:

Housekeeping aids
    broom
    bucket
    mop
    sponge
Cooking/eating tools
    dishes
    pans
    plastic food
    "silverware"

Toddlers practice combining materials and objects but may not be planning to make anything in particular. However, by experimenting with materials, toddlers and 2-year-olds discover the means by which materials can be combined and how the results look when finished.

Full of skills, energy, imagination, and curiosity, the preschooler is a learning-playing dynamo.

Helping Preschoolers
Play: Three to 5 Years

The preschool years are perhaps the most playful ones of all childhood. The preschooler is skilled with his or her body, with language, and with peers. With these skills, energy, imagination, and curiosity, the preschooler is a learning-playing dynamo. When we provide toys, materials, some timely guidance, and above all time for play, we enhance the development at this stage.

The preschooler's fundamental movement abilities continue to develop along with refinement of manipulative abilities. Preschoolers practice mental skills that involve sorting, matching, naming, and ordering. They also play with words and sounds, experimenting with new sounds and word combinations. And they practice asking questions: Why? Why? Why? Suggestions for providing experiences and materials for preschoolers are:

• Provide a variety of toys and equipment to challenge gross motor skills. Preschoolers need vehicles for riding, balls for throwing and catching, and space for hopping, running, twisting, turning, dancing, tumbling, and rolling. There should be equipment for climbing, swinging, balancing, sliding, pedaling, hauling, digging, and building.

• Arrange for many toys and materials to develop fine motor skills. Provide objects for stacking, pushing, pulling, throwing, punching, fitting together, building, and activating. Provide materials and tools for practicing cutting, drawing, writing, coloring, painting, tying, lacing, buttoning, snapping, zipping, and fastening.

Stimulate dramatic play by providing a variety of props and plenty of experiences for children to pretend about.

- Offer lots of materials for practicing mental skills such as matching, sorting, ordering, listening, naming, and rearranging.

  ~lay singing games such as Mulberry Bush and Ring
  ` ~ Rosy.

Pretend play

Preschoolers usually pretend or dramatize events with their playmates—hence the term sociodramatic play. They act out more complex dramas with more events, roles, and object substitutions than do toddlers.

- Add more variety to the props available. The housekeeping area needs tools for complex cooking scenarios, including preparing and cooking pretend food and arranging the table. Add to the ones provided for toddlers such props as:

      pancake turners
      rotary beaters
      bowls
      baking sheets
      rolling pins
      muffin tins
      measuring cups
      measuring spoons
      aprons
      tablecloths
      centerpieces
      colorful napkins

- Props do not need to be as realistic as for earlier ages. Model airplanes, buses, cars, boats, trains, and construction vehicles need not have detailed features. Ambiguity allows children to fill in the details as to which types of vehicles are in use. Children will also use everyday items for creative purposes: A block could be a microphone for a rock singer and a moment later a bone for a dog.

• Provide a variety of props to symbolize roles of family members and community workers. Use hats, uniforms, and tools of the trade to symbolize roles. Keep a collection organized into containers for each role. Here are some examples:

Hats/costumes/uniforms for:

women
men
babies
chefs
ranchers
mail carriers
police
drivers
construction workers
farmers
astronauts
divers
soldiers
doctors
nurses
dentists
news reporters
ship captains

Other role symbols:

crowns for kings, queens, princesses, princes
sweat bands for aerobics teachers/students
microphones for singers
headphones for disc jockeys
costumes for storybook characters/animals

• In addition to role symbols, children need objects or substitute objects that symbolize the *actions* carried out in various roles. Examples of objects needed are:

    paper and pencils for almost all roles
    books for librarian
    cash register, cash, merchandise for storekeeper
    buses, taxis, ships, planes for drivers
    records and microphone for disc jockey
    cameras for photographers
    typewriters for secretaries
    envelopes, mailbag, postal boxes for mail carrier
    tickets, animal models, cages for zookeeper
    hair rollers, dryer, brushes, wigs for hair stylist

• Children symbolize roles, objects, and *events*. Many events will be enacted by preschoolers experienced enough in dramatic play to carry out a drama with several sequences. Be sure to let children choose the theme(s). Here are some examples:

    beach vacation
    camping
    making a movie/video
    living at the circus
    going on a trip to _____
    going to Oz (or other storybook adventure)

• Become a participant in the drama when needed. Sometimes an adult is needed to be the patient for the doctor, the rider on a bus, the customer at the bakery, or the receiver of letters.

- Provide puppets and a stage. Older preschoolers will enjoy putting on a puppet show for an audience of playmates or teachers. Puppets are especially good for depicting favorite stories.

- Read children books with colorful, memorable language that they can use in their plays, such as "I'll huff and I'll puff and I'll blow your house down."

Take children on field trips to see people in various roles. Try a hospital, a firehouse, a grocery store. Provide the props to enact the roles.

Building and making play

Preschoolers are excellent builders and makers and spend much time creating. Ways to support this play are:
- Make available several choices of constructive activities during free choice time. Constructive materials for this age include such items as:

unit blocks (wooden)

blocks of various sizes and materials

boards

large building materials (tires to stack, boxes, barrels, pillows, large foam shapes)

interlocking plastic manipulatives

sand (Provide molding shapes, shovel, scoops, cups.)

mud (Provide scoops, molds, water, and clean-up supplies.)

water (Provide containers, tubes, pumps, measuring cups, and things to wash.)

plumbing pipes to put together and take apart

large beads to string

puzzles (Provide a variety with various numbers of pieces. Provide some whole-piece puzzles and some interlocking puzzles.)

parquetry blocks for designs

cooking supplies and equipment (Use simple recipes with few ingredients and little waiting time until tasting for young preschoolers. Older preschoolers can measure, mix, and wait for something to cook.)

- Use words for constructing songs, stories, and poems. Let children dictate stories and poems as you write them down, then read them to the children.

Building and making projects give children opportunities to express their boundless creativity.

Helping Primary Age Children Play: Six to 8 Years

Primary age children are increasingly competent players. Bike riders, skateboarders, play stagers, lemonade stand owners—they demonstrate skill and sophistication. At the same time they are becoming competent workers; their work in our society is being a student. A dichotomy between work and play develops in children's minds during these years, encouraged by the school.

Play in elementary school

The elementary school is typically so demanding in its requirements for curriculum and behavior that both teachers and children are governed by a work ethic. Classroom teachers convinced of the value of play thus find incorporating play into the young child's day a challenge. Some of the ways teachers can help children experience play are:

● Allow choices whenever possible. This grants some freedom, an essential for play. Arrange curriculum to support diversity rather than conformity in learning styles. Arrange curriculum so that variety in sequencing is possible—most things do not have to be learned according to a curriculum guide's scope and sequence chart. Furthermore, most children actively seek challenge and when allowed to choose will seek a difficult task that has reasonable possibility of success.

- Keep the focus on the process—not the outcome. Integrate reading, mathematics, and spelling into student-chosen projects. Many projects—building something, putting on a play, doing community service—provide opportunities for practicing basic academic skills. Thad chose to make a book for his younger sister's birthday gift. In the process he asked for and received help in spelling several words and learning how to punctuate his story. When finished, he practiced reading the work. When children acquire basic academic skills in a setting in which they choose the level of difficulty and have control over the topic, learning is fun. This approach establishes the basis for a lifelong love of learning.

- Provide "free time" when children can choose from a variety of enjoyable activities such as games, manipulatives, art materials, and puzzles.

- Allow ample opportunity for children to use newly acquired reading and writing skills to create stories, jokes, poems, and books. Young schoolchildren enjoy practicing mental skills such as answering riddles, telling jokes, making up stories, reading, and solving problems. Listen to jokes and write stories down.

- Encourage children to dramatize stories, novels, social studies, and science learnings. Allow children to spend several days if necessary to plan dramas, negotiate roles, and build scenery. Help them find, make, and improvise props. School-age children enjoy putting on dramas for an audience—especially for younger children. Do not expect them to memorize lines—the drama is likely to change each time it is rehearsed or presented. Children may improvise new episodes as the play progresses, with a few time-outs to decide what will happen next. Relax and enjoy the production. Let the children be the directors. If a play becomes bogged down, prompt by leading phrases such as "And then he _____," or "The next day when she woke up she_____," or "This made her feel_____." If it seems wise to end the drama, summarize and then end with "And ever after that, they_____," or "And they lived happily for a long time."

• Display projects for others (parents, peers, younger groups) to see.

• Provide film, tapes, and equipment for creating photo essays, filmstrips, videos, and sound productions.

• Provide space and equipment for large motor activities.

• Provide a psychologically safe environment for the practice of emerging skills. To feel psychologically secure, confident, and full of self-esteem, children need acceptance from adults and peers and experiences of success—projects that are not too difficult to master, yet challenging enough to be interesting.

Primary-grade children learn better through games and projects that use all their skills and knowledge together than by studying isolated subjects by means of "instruction" and paperwork.

Play in other settings

Adults responsible for children in other settings—homes, camps, after-school programs, and centers—have far greater latitude in encouraging children's play. The suggestions for teachers can be extended to include:

• Allow the widest possible choice for projects. Children like to make real things at this stage. Woodworking, puppetry, pottery, and bookmaking provide chances for real construction.

• Allow more time for planning and provide guidance (when asked) on possible outcomes. Schoolchildren will spend more time planning, shopping, and anticipating the outcome of a tie-dye T-shirt project than younger children will on a tie-dye scarf.

• Older children often spend several days on constructive projects. Space is needed to store projects when they will extend into another day. When facilities are shared with other groups, locked cabinets may be necessary to protect constructions in progress. Sometimes the display of a warning sign is sufficient.

• Do not compare or grade constructions. Do not hold competitions or offer rewards. This takes the focus off the fun of skill acquisition. Seeing the finished product provides feedback and serves as its own reward.

• Furnish complex puzzles with interlocking pieces. School-age children often work together on complex puzzles that take several days to complete.

• Vary the levels of difficulty (number and complexity of puzzle pieces, for example) so children can choose activities that challenge but do not frustrate them.

After-school programs should offer children variety and opportunities to practice their favorite skills.

Arrange materials, space, and time for further refinement of fine motor skills such as stringing beads, working puzzles (smaller pieces and more pieces than for preschoolers), cutting, writing, sewing (large needles, thread, and surfaces—no patterns), drawing, and constructing crafts.

• Provide materials, space, and time for practicing and playing games that involve large motor skills such as skipping, tumbling, jumping, running, climbing, and balancing. Biking, skating, and skateboarding are currently popular. Skills acquired in earlier years need to continue— swimming, for example.

• Make the environment physically safe. This includes a safe, fenced-in playground with safe equipment and break-fall surfaces. It also means setting and enforcing safety rules—both indoors and outdoors.

• Design cooking projects that involve more complex recipes than in the preschool years (more ingredients, more steps in combining ingredients, more accuracy in measuring). Young school-age children are able to wait longer to taste the finished product so recipes that require time to rise, set, cook, or freeze will be more acceptable at this age.

• Allow experimentation with creating new recipes so children learn how different combinations produce different results. Provide guidance in planning so that the waste of food is minimal, but let children be free to try things new ways. When it seems likely that the cooked product will be inedible, guide children to experiment with small quantities so less food is wasted.

Keep games for preschoolers simple and focus on the fun of playing, not on winning or losing.

Playing Games

G ames are a familiar and obvious kind of play. We play Peek-a-Boo with the baby and Monopoly™ with the second grader. As children grow so does their ability to master rules and plan strategies. Similarly, their social interaction skills increase because games require mutual involvement, role reciprocity, and turn taking. Although we often think of games as being competitive, with winning and losing the outcome, actually much cooperation is required to play games. Development of this cooperativeness is a principal value of game playing for children.

When thinking about games for children, we should keep several principles in mind.

Principles for games

• Participation in games must always be voluntary. When participation is forced, resistance and rebellion instead of cooperation are likely to result.

• Reduce competitiveness.

1. Keep the focus on the fun of playing, not on winning. Comment on the skills or the fun, but do not give unusual attention to the winners. "You really made a clever move that time," or "You had fun playing that game, didn't you?" should be sufficient.

2. Do not offer prizes or rewards to winners. This puts the focus back on the winning rather than on the development of skills. It also takes away from the development of self-motivation.

3. Handle competition carefully. Competition that requires players to figure out the opponent's strategy helps children become aware of others' views. However, the focus should be on sharpening skills—not on winning. Some children need help accepting that it is all right to lose. Point out the good moves or skills they used. Children who do not wish to enter into competition might be allowed to "just watch." Games that depend on luck might be less threatening to some children because they don't show up their weaknesses. Kamii and DeVries (1980) in the book *Group Games in Early Education* provide excellent suggestions on handling competition.

• Keep children active. Do not have a group that must sit out and watch others play after they have lost or made an error. This puts focus on the mistake and can contribute to a loss of self-esteem. Also, it is just plain boring to sit and watch while others have fun. In games such as musical chairs, provide another activity for children to go to when they are eliminated or change the game so no one is left out. Just remove the chair or carpet square being used but let all players continue.

• Choose teams in ways that neither sex stereotype nor damage self-esteem. If you were ever the last to be chosen for a team, you know the feeling of rejection. Children who have that experience repeatedly may develop low self-esteem, or a dislike of group activities. Organize teams by drawing straws (two colors), or by the number of letters in first names (odd number on one team, even on the other). What other ways can you think of?

- Keep flexible on rules.
  1. Introduce rules gradually. Simplify games when you first introduce them, using only a few of the rules. Add more rules later to make the game more challenging. Older children can remember and abide by more rules than can younger ones.
  2. Allow children to change the rules so long as they agree on the changes. The process of working out the changes is important in developing social skills.
- First games should be success experiences. When first learning to play games, children need to "win" a few rounds. This requires a mature play partner—an adult or older and more mature child who can be flexible about the way the game is played, including adapting the rules.
- Consider skills of the players.
  1. When children of widely differing skill levels play, offer games with an element of chance. This equalizes the possibilities for winning. Adults can find playing games with children challenging when chance heightens the suspense. It provides children with a sense of equality with adults—at least in the play setting.
  2. Select games that require skills appropriate to the children's level of development. Games that are too easy are boring; those that are too difficult are frustrating. The children themselves are the best judges of which games are challenging but fun. Provide a variety of choices so they can choose the ones that challenge and interest them.

Older children enjoy complex games with rules they may negotiate or invent for themselves.

PLAYING GAMES

Preschool years (3-, 4-, and 5-year-olds). Preschoolers enjoy noncompetitive guessing games, simple board games, and simple card games that use skills for recognizing, matching, and ordering numbers, colors, shapes, sizes, textures, and familiar objects. Simple games of chasing, racing, and aiming (musical chairs, bean bag toss, tag, and shadow tag) combine and use motor skills. Adult supervision of games is needed to remind children how to play the game and to give active hints about how to "win." You can introduce board games if they use only a few simple rules that can be relaxed to let the child "win."

School age (grades K–3). At this age children become quite adept at playing games that involve anticipating the opponent's strategy. Thus, sports and complex board games with several rules are popular among this age group. Children view rules as important; if a playmate breaks a rule, the friendship may be lost, at least temporarily. With experience in playing by the rules, children begin to bargain for changes in rules and may develop some interesting new games. Do not interfere with the bargaining—that's an important part of the learning. Sometimes children spend so much time trying to settle on the rules, they never get around to playing the game. After experience with commercial versions, given materials, children can create their own board games.

Using conversation to play with ideas can expand children's thinking.

Making Nonplay More Playful

A child's day isn't all play, but the more playful it is, the higher the quality of life. Thus, even activities we don't think of as play—conversation, reading, and transitions— lend themselves to playfulness if a teacher or child wishes so. Talking and reading were included in the suggestions for supporting play; here is a fuller discussion of the play aspects of these activities, and some observations on transitions. We also include some suggestions for the special problems of the nonplaying child.

Conversation

Talking with adults and playmates is an important means of language development. A lot of learning takes place when adults answer endless questions and share their own experiences, insights, and feelings. How is conversation related to play? First, it uses some of the rules for play—mutual involvement, turn taking, and reciprocity. Both partners listen and share—no one always leads, no one always follows. Second, it can be used to play with words, ideas, and fantasies.

How adults talk with children is important. Adults need to be sensitive to the child's mood. A negative mood may reflect anger, frustration, or sadness. A stressed or unhappy child cannot be playful. If the child seems anxious, or upset in some way, the adult should offer a secure base and good

Children will be interested in writing if they are free to express their own interests, not if they're worried about "getting it right."

listening skills. Gordon's (1970) book *Parent Effectiveness Training* provides information on how to listen for feelings in a way that promotes feelings of acceptance and security, which are necessary in order for play to occur. So even when the mood is negative, there is an opportunity to meet the needs that must be met in order to play.

Sometimes the mood may be one in which the child searches for answers to questions about life and death, how things work, what the future might be like, and what would happen if_____?

When the mood is light, conversation can be used to "play" with ideas. Encourage the children to think creatively. Ask questions such as "If you could go on a trip to anywhere you wanted and to as many places as you wanted, where would you go?" Encourage the children to think of as many places as possible. Contribute your own ideas too. "Could we stop at_____and get some _____?" Don't be afraid to pretend to go to Jupiter and Mars and beyond the galaxy. Imagine what it will be like. "What will you need to take?" Ask questions like "Where else?" "What else?" "How else?" "Who else?" as ways to stimulate thinking of as many ideas as possible.

As you talk with children, use the opportunity to find out about their thinking. What are they concerned about? What are their interests? In what areas do they seem to lack some understanding? Use this information to plan for new books, activities, field trips, and experiences.

Reading

Reading can be playful when it is under the child's control. The child has choice about what to read and also chooses the level of difficulty of the material. Provide a variety of reading materials on various topics and at various levels of difficulty. Some books can be pictures only, others pictures and words. Reading is also a playful experience if adults write down the child's story and read it or allow the child to read it, depending on the child's level of development. Writing their own stories is playful if the focus is on each child expressing her interests. It is not play if there is anxiety over the story being marked for spelling, grammar, and handwriting.

Transitions

Setting up, cleaning up, and changing from one activity to another are all transitions. Transitions are necessary but they interrupt play; therefore, there should be as few as possible during the day. If children have had plenty of time to explore, play, and finish projects, they will be better able to stop the activity to clean up or move on to another scheduled event. It is also easier for them if they have had a warning that play time is about to end: "Five minutes until cleanup." Some teachers dim lights or ring a bell to signal cleanup. More playful teachers turn cleanup into pretense or use a song/game approach. One teacher uses a freeze-music gamelike approach. Each child tries to see how many things he or she can put away before the music stops and everyone freezes in position for 5 seconds until music starts again.

Let children have fun getting messy, and help them have fun cleaning up. A warning a few minutes before it's time to change activities lets children know what to expect.

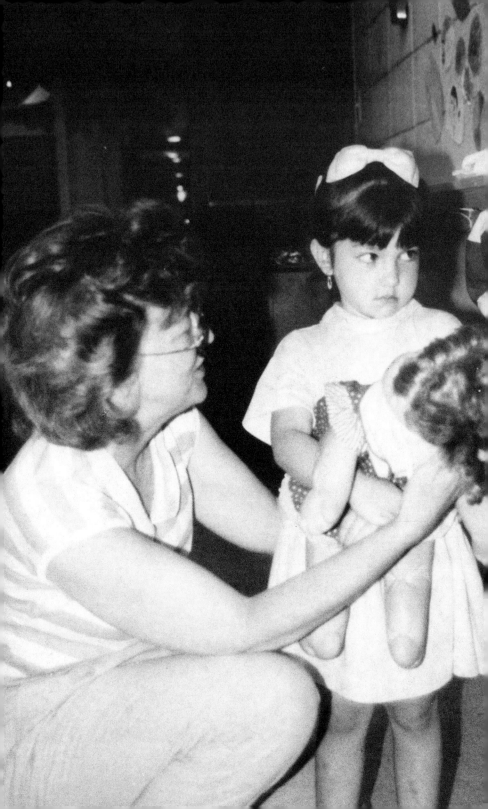

Make a special effort to help shy and rejected children join in the play.

The nonplaying child

When children are unable to join in play, observe and try to determine the reason. Are there enough interesting activities from which to choose? Does the child feel accepted and secure with the adults and peers in the setting? Is the child shy? Determine the possible cause and then set about correcting it. Provide more activities. Make a special effort to help the insecure child know he can trust you to provide comfort when needed. Help the shy child find a special friend or select an activity near other children. Give the neglected/rejected child a special task to do that will be valued by others.

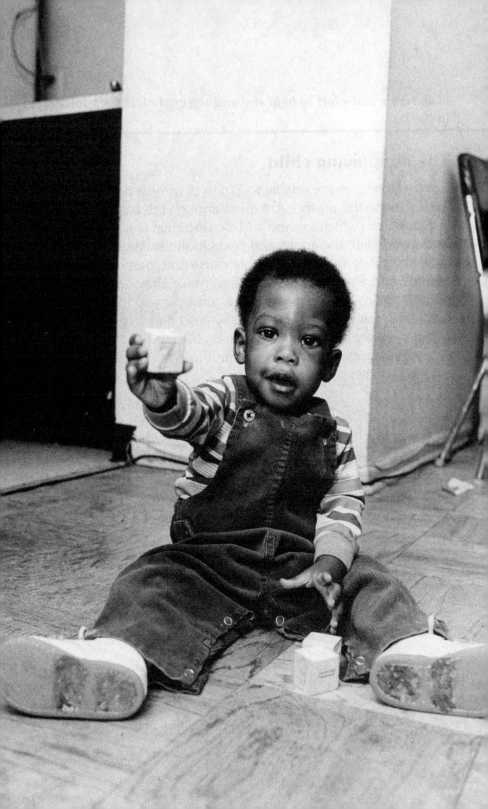

In Conclusion

This book explains how play is related to development and what adults can do to support play. A century of research and experience has shown us that play is the foundation for children's healthy development. Development occurs in an orderly sequence. Children's play shows us how well they are developing and is also the means for further development. It helps children develop knowledge, social skills, and motor skills. It also helps them express feelings appropriately. Thus, play is the basis of developmentally appropriate programs for young children.

Although play is natural for young children, adults have a major role in assuring that children derive the known benefits of play for fostering all kinds of development—mental, social, emotional, and physical. As parents and teachers we make a difference in children's play by how we interact with the children and how we arrange settings in which they are inclined to play. Quite possibly the most difficult work teachers have to do in implementing a high-quality play program is teaching the parents, decision makers, and coworkers that play is a whole lot more than "just" play.

Resources

Resources for supporting play

Baker, K. R. (1966). *Let's play outdoors*. Washington, DC: NAEYC.

Cherry, C. (1972). *Creative art for the developing child*. Belmont, CA: Pitman Learning.

Cherry, C. (1971). *Creative movement for the developing child: A nursery handbook for non-musicians*. Belmont, CA: Pitman Learning.

Hill, D. M. (1977). *Mud, sand, and water*. Washington, DC: NAEYC.

Hirsch, E. S. (Ed.). (1984). *The block book* (rev. ed.). Washington, DC: NAEYC.

Hunt, T., & Renfro, N. (1982). *Puppetry in early childhood education*. Austin, TX: Nancy Renfro Studios.

Lasky, L., & Mukerji, R. (1980). *Art: Basic for young children*. Washington, DC: NAEYC.

Manning, K., & Sharp, A. (1977). *Structuring play in the early years at school*. London: Ward Lock Educational in association with Drake Educational Associates.

McCaslin, N. (1975). *Act now! Plays and ways to make them*. New York: S. G. Phillips.

McDonald, D. T. (1979). *Music in our lives: The early years*. Washington, DC: NAEYC.

National Association for the Education of Young Children. (1985). *Toys: Tools for learning*. Washington, DC: Author.

Schirrmacher, R. (1986). Talking with young children about their art. *Young Children, 41*(5), 3–7.

Skeen, P., Garner, A. P., & Cartwright, S. (1984). *Woodworking for young children.* Washington, DC: NAEYC.

Sullivan, M. (1982). *Feeling strong, feeling free: Movement exploration for young children.* Washington, DC: NAEYC.

Sutton-Smith, B., & Sutton-Smith, S. (1974). *How to play with your children (and when not to).* New York: Hawthorn/ Dutton.

Wanamaker, N., Hearn, K., & Richarz, S. (1979). *More than graham crackers: Nutrition education and food preparation with young children.* Washington, DC: NAEYC.

Resources for supporting games

Block, J. H., & King, N. R. (1987). *School play: A source book.* New York: Garland.

Bogdanoff, R. F., & Dolch, E. T. (1979). *Old games for young children: A link to our heritage.* Young Children, 34(2), 37–45.

Fluegelman, A. (Ed.). (1976). *The new games book.* New York: Dolphin.

Fluegelman, A. (1981). *More new games.* New York: Dolphin.

Kamii, C., & DeVries, R. (1980). *Group games in early education: Implications of Piaget's theory.* Washington, DC: NAEYC.

Resources for making nonplay more playful

Supporting conversation

Cazden, C. B. (Ed.). (1981). *Language in early childhood education* (rev. ed.). Washington, DC: NAEYC.

Gordon, T. (1970). *Parent effectiveness training.* New York: Wyden.

Zavitkovsky, D., Baker, K. R., Berlfein, J. R., & Almy, M. (1986). *Listen to the children.* Washington, DC: NAEYC.

Reading

Lamme, L. L. (1984). *Growing up writing.* Washington, DC: Acropolis.

Rogers, C. S., & Wolfle, J. A. (1981). Foundations for literacy: A building blocks model. *Young Children, 36*(2), 26–32.

Schickedanz, J. A. (1986). *More than the ABCs: The early stages of reading and writing.* Washington, DC: NAEYC.

Transitions

Alger, H. A. (1984). Transitions: Alternatives to manipulative management techniques. *Young Children, 39*(6), 16–25.

Helping a nonplayer join players

Roopnarine, J. L., & Honig, A. S. (1985). Research in review. The unpopular child. *Young Children, 40*(6), 59–64.

Trawick-Smith, J. (1988). "Let's say you're the baby, OK?" Play leadership and following behavior in young children. *Young Children, 43*(5), 51–59.

References

Gordon, T. (1970). *Parent effectiveness training.* New York: Wyden.

Kamii, C., & DeVries, R. (1980). *Group games in early education: Implications of Piaget's theory.* Washington, DC: NAEYC.

Levy, J. (1978). *Play behavior.* New York: Wiley.

Tizard, B. (1977). Play: The child's way of learning? In B. Tizard & D. Harvey (Eds.), *Biology of play* (pp. 199–208). Philadelphia: Lippincott.